Workplace Spanish® for
RESTAURANT & FOOD SERVICE

TABLE OF CONTENTS

Workplace Spanish, Inc. // Roswell, GA 30076 // www.WorkplaceSpanish.com

¡BIENVENIDOS!

THE WORKPLACE SPANISH® MISSION

The Hispanic population of the United States is growing at an unprecedented rate!

- In the past 10-years the Hispanic population has grown 4 times faster than the US population as a whole.

- Currently 1 of every 7 people in the US is Hispanic – that's 40 million Hispanics!

- Over the next 10 years, Hispanics will account for 44% of the US population growth.

This phenomenal growth presents great opportunities and difficult challenges for employers who must communicate with Spanish-speaking employees, customers, and citizens. Organizations can improve teamwork & productivity with Spanish training, but today's adult workers don't have the time to learn Spanish in the traditional way.

That's why we developed Workplace Spanish® — to help you communicate, simply but effectively, at work, in Spanish!

Our job-specific programs use bite-size terms and phrases, easy phonetic pronunciations, and carefully selected expressions that you can *learn today and use tomorrow*. Our programs do not require grammar, verb conjugations or complicated language rules. No prior Spanish experience is necessary!

PROGRAM OBJECTIVES

1. To introduce you to Latin American Spanish language and pronunciation.

2. To help you learn, pronounce, and use workplace expressions ------- **in Spanish**.

3. To build your confidence to *"Say it in Spanish"* ----- so you can communicate with Latino employees and co-workers in a basic but effective manner.

BENEFITS YOU CAN ACHIEVE

- Improved communication and teamwork between co-workers

- Clearer instructions resulting in better efficiency & safety

- Fewer accidents and quality mistakes

- Less employee frustration and lower turnover

- Increased skill set for Hispanic employees

- Higher quality service to Hispanic customers

LEARNING SUGGESTIONS

A Workplace Spanish® materials will help you communicate quickly, simply & effectively. Unlike a textbook, each topic is independent and does not require knowledge of other topics. Don't tackle the entire manual – work your way through one section at a time.

B Listening to your CD while driving is a quick way to practice pronunciation and learn new material. **Pick out a single topic and concentrate on those expressions** – this is much more effective than skipping around the CD. We do NOT recommend listening to the entire CD at one time – it is boring and not very productive.

C Our CDs are unique. They feature both a native speaker and an American pronouncing the Spanish phrases. For the best results, repeat the Spanish phrases WITH THE AMERICAN SPEAKER.

GOLDEN RULES FOR GREAT RESULTS

1. BROWSE – through the manual to understand its organization – 1) Introduction; 2)Topics & Expressions; 3) Practice Conversations; 4) Drills for Skills; 5) Alphabetical Keyword List

2. READ – through the Introduction section, paying careful attention to the pages on pronunciation. Listen to the Spanish pronunciation on the CD and practice until you begin to become comfortable. If you are new to Spanish, learn how to use the phonetic column as an aid to pronunciation. Pronounce the syllables S-L-O-W-L-Y!

3. BEGIN – with the Meeting & Greeting expressions. These are very important and you can practice them anywhere. Listen to the expressions on the CD while looking at the manual. Repeat them out loud ALONG WITH the American voice on the CD.

4. PRIORITIZE – everything in this manual is <u>NOT</u> of equal importance – YOU must decide what is most important to you. Identify & prioritize those topics that you will use most frequently. Master them first – save the other material for reference.

5. PRACTICE ALOUD – with family, co-workers, customers. The most difficult hurdle to overcome is becoming confident enough to say things aloud in Spanish. Practicing aloud will give you the confidence to use Spanish in work situations. The practice conversations will help you get the feel of back & forth dialogue with Hispanics.

6. TEST YOURSELF – listen to the CD to check your pronunciation. Spend time on your priority topics. Use the "Drills for Skills" section to test your knowledge.

7. SET A GOAL – even if it's only one phrase a day – learn something new every day. In a month you can easily master 30 to 60 expressions. What's your goal?

CULTURE TIPS

1. "Latino" and "Hispanic" are both correct terms for the Spanish speaking population of the Caribbean, Central and South America. Hispanics come from 20 different countries.

2. "Hispanic" is not a race – it is an ethnic origin! It is a term that was created by the Census Bureau. Hispanics (Latinos) come from Spanish ancestry – from Spaniards who explored Central & South America and the Caribbean. Many settled there and married Indians who were native to the areas -- creating a culture that is both diverse and rich in tradition.

3. Latinos immigrate to the US to earn enough money to build a better life for their families. Sometimes the families stay behind and the workers live together – often 8 to 10 in a small apartment. Frequently, they send much of their paycheck home to their families.

4. There is a high illiteracy rate among entry-level Latino workers. Often, these workers are unable to read Spanish and cannot understand written English. Using the basic Spanish from this program will enable you to cut through the language barrier.

5. In Spanish, dates are usually written with the day first, followed by the month and year -- using periods instead of commas, as Europeans do. Thus, July 9, 2003 would be written as 09.07.03 by a Latino. Remember this when talking about dates & schedules.

6. Latin Americans write their financial numbers differently – notice the use of commas and periods in this example: $1,002.08 dollars would be written as 1.002,08 by a Latino.

7. Hispanics frequently have 4 or 5 names, including a first name, middle name and 2 last names. Their mother's maiden name usually comes after the father's family name.

   Thus in the US, José Marco Ramirez Gavrón would be José M. Ramirez. Cecilia Maria Sanchez Ramirez would be Cecilia M. Sanchez.

8. Don't confuse shyness with dishonesty; Latinos usually do not make direct eye contact with their supervisors. This is both a cultural trait and a sign of respect.

9. Hispanic employees and customers are very loyal. They need to be treated with respect and feel they are part of the team – just like anyone else. They work hard and can benefit from good basic instructions and clear explanations of the things they don't understand.

10. Keeping one's job and maintaining a steady paycheck are of paramount importance – because of this, be aware that some accidents or mistakes may go unreported.

LANGUAGE TIPS

SHORTER IS EASIER!

1. Unless you're a diplomat or rocket scientist, you'll find that shorter is better. It's much easier to say 4 or 5 words than 10 or 12. The purpose of this program is to help you get your point across or understand someone else – not to be fluent.

2. Saying a few words in Spanish demonstrates respect for the Latino culture – watch the smiles that you get when you say (or try to say) something to a Latino in Spanish.

3. The speed of Hispanic conversation is "rápido"! Mastering the following expressions early will help reduce your frustration: "Más despacio" (slower) and "Repita eso" (repeat that).

MASCULINE & FEMININE

4. Unlike English, Spanish classifies its nouns as either masculine or feminine. Adjectives and articles (like the word "the") change according to the gender of the noun. In general nouns ending in "a" are feminine and have "la" or "una" in front of them.

   Nouns ending in "o" are generally masculine and have "el" or "un" in front of them. But there are many exceptions, so we have chosen not to dwell on this. If you say "martillo" instead of "el martillo", a Latino will still know that you mean hammer.

5. Certain nouns change when referring to a woman. For example "el gerente" (the manager) would become "la gerente" for a woman.

6. Some examples of "normal" nouns are: "la casa" (the house) and "el carro" (the car). But it can be confusing when you run into "la mano" (the hand) or "el mapa" (the map). For this reason, we have eliminated the use of many articles throughout the program.

PLURAL NOUNS & ACCENT MARKS

7. Nouns, adjectives, and articles ending in a vowel become plural by adding an "s". For example, "la casa" (house) becomes "las casas" and "el bombero" (fireman) becomes "los bomberos". Nouns, adjectives and articles **ending in a consonant** usually add "es", so *camión* (truck) becomes *camiones, señor* (sir or mister) becomes *señores,* and *supervisor* (supervisor) becomes *supervisores.*

8. Accent marks are used frequently in Spanish - they are a guide to pronunciation. The syllable containing an accent mark is stressed when you pronounce the Spanish word. For example, Información has stress on the last syllable – different than in English.

9. All this can be confusing, but remember that you can usually convey your meaning in a few words. Take your time and pronounce the words slowly until you become comfortable and confident. Don't let a concern for grammar get in the way of communication.

SPANISH PRONUNCIATION

Spanish words you probably know :

americano	amigo	bandido	burrito
cerveza	cha-cha	chiquita	dinero
fiesta	grande	gringo	jefe
latino	mucho	pueblo	rancho
río	rodeo	siesta	tequila

NOTE: These words demonstrate most of the sounds in the Spanish language. Refer to this list for easy examples of Spanish pronunciation.

Vowels – Unlike English, all vowels are pronounced in Spanish:

Vowel	Spanish Sound	Sounds Like:	Spanish word	Pronunciation
A	ah	ah choo	amigo	ah-**mee**-go
E	eh or ay	elephant / stay	verde	**behr**-day
I	ee	meet	prima	**pree**-ma
O	oh	oh no / okay	poco	**po**-ko
U	oo	moo	seguro	seh-**goo**-roh
Y	ee	meet	y *(and)*	**ee**

Consonants – These consonants sound different in Spanish than in English:

Letter	Spanish Sound	Sounds Like:	Spanish word	Pronunciation
CH	Always soft	church / cha cha	chalupa	cha-**loo**-pah
H	Always silent	N/A in English	hola	**oh**-lah
J	Sounds like H	hello	jabón	hah-**bone**
LL	Sounds like Y or J	N/A in English	llamo	**yah**-mo / **jah**-mo
Ñ	Sounds like NY	canyon	español	ess-pahn-**yole**
QU	Sounds like K	OK	que	kay
RR	Trilled (repeated)	N/A in English	sierra	see-**air**-rah
V	Can sound like either B or V	English is normal V sound	ventana	ben-**tah**-nah / ven-**tah**-nah
Z	Sounds like 's'	soft	zapatos	sah-**pah**-tohs

PHONETIC PRONUNCIATION

1. On each page the Spanish words are broken down into syllables to help you pronounce them properly. These "phonetic shortcuts" will make it easier for you to pronounce the word and be understood. Be sure to place more stress on the syllables in **bold type**.

2. As you can see from the examples below, Spanish words are often separated into more syllables than their English counterparts. **When starting pronounce slowly** – syllable by syllable – then gradually build up your speed through repetition! **The biggest mistake most people make is trying to pronounce the syllables too quickly.**

3. DASHES indicate SEPARATE SYLLABLES! SLASHES indicate SEPARATE WORDS! Phonetic pronunciations make it easier for you to speak Spanish and be understood. They are NOT meant to make you a perfect speaker.

PRONUNCIATION EXAMPLES

SPANISH & ENGLISH WORDS		PHONETIC PRONUNCIATION
English word:	Information	in-for-**may**-shun
Spanish word:	Información	een-for-mah-see-**own**
English word:	Police	puh-**lease**
Spanish word:	Policía	po-lee-**see**-ah
English word:	Supervisor	**super**-vie-ser
Spanish word:	Supervisor	soo-pair-bee-**soar**

SPANISH EXPRESSIONS	PHONETIC PRONUNCIATION
Hablo un poco de español	ah-blow / oon / **po**-ko / day / ess-pahn-**yole**
No comprendo	no / comb-**pren**-doe
¿Cómo está hoy?	**ko**-mo / ess-**tah** / oy
Repita eso, por favor	ray-**pee**-tah / **ess**-oh / por / fah-**boar**

MEETING & GREETING

GREETINGS

Hello	Hola	**oh**-lah
Good morning	Buenos días	**bway**-nose / **dee**-ahs
Good afternoon	Buenas tardes	**bway**-nahs / **tar**-days
Good evening	Buenas noches	**bway**-nahs / **no**-chess
Can I help you?	¿Le puedo ayudar?	lay / **pway**-doe / ah-you-**dahr**
Just a minute	Un momento	oon / mo-**men**-toe
Are you looking for work?	Está buscando trabajo?	ess-**tah** / boo-**skahn**-doe / tra-**bah**-ho
What type of work?	¿Qué tipo de trabajo?	kay / **tee**-poe / day / tra-**bah**-ho

INTRODUCTIONS

What's your name?	¿Cómo se llama?	**ko**-mo / say / **yah**-mah
My name is...	*Me llamo...*	may / **yah**-mo...
I'm the manager	Soy el jefe // Soy la jefa	soy / el / **heh**-fay // soy / lah / **heh**-fah
I'm the shift manager	Soy el jefe de turno	soy / el / **heh**-fay / day / **toor**-no
How are you?	¿Cómo está?	**ko**-mo / ess-**tah**
Very well, thank you	*Muy bien, gracias*	mwee / bee-**yen** / **grah**-see-ahs
And you?	*¿Y usted?*	ee / oo-**sted**
Nice to meet you	Mucho gusto	**moo**-cho / **goose**-toe
Please sit down	Siéntese, por favor	see-**en**-tay-say / pore / fah-**boar**

POLITE PHRASES

Excuse me	Disculpe // Perdone	dee-**school**-pay // pair-**doan**-ay
I'm sorry	Lo siento	lo / see-**en**-toe
Miss // Mrs.	Señorita // Señora	sen-yore-**ree**-tah // sen-**yore**-ah
Mister // Sir	Señor	sen-**yore**
Please	Por favor	pore / fah-**boar**
Thank you (very much)	(Muchas) gracias	(**moo**-chahs) **grah**-see-ahs
You're welcome	De nada	day / **nah**-dah
How are you today?	¿Cómo está hoy?	**ko**-mo / ess-**tah** / oy
Are things going well?	¿Está todo bien?	ess-**tah** / **toe**-doe / bee-**en**
Is something wrong?	¿Algo está mal?	**ahl**-go / ess-**tah** / mahl

LANGUAGE EXPRESSIONS & FAMILY

SPEAKING ENGLISH & SPANISH		
Do you speak English?	¿Habla inglés?	**ah**-blah / een-**glace**
Do you understand?	¿Comprende? OR ¿Entiende?	comb-**pren**-day OR en-tee-**en**-day
I don't understand	No comprendo	no / comb-**pren**-doe
I speak a little Spanish	Hablo un poco de español	**ah**-blow / oon / **po**-ko / day ess-pahn-**yole**
Repeat that please	Repita eso, por favor	ray-**pee**-tah / **ess**-so / pore / fah-**boar**
Slower (please)	Más despacio (por favor)	**mahs** / day-**spa**-see-oh (pore / fah-**boar**)
Tell me in English	Dígame en inglés	**dee**-gah-may / en / een-**glace**
What did you say?	¿Cómo? OR ¿Qué dijo?	**ko**-mo OR kay / **dee**-ho
What is this in Spanish?	¿Cómo se dice esto en español?	**ko**-mo / say / **dee**-say / **ess**-toe / en / ess-pahn-**yole**
Write it, please	Escríbalo, por favor	ess-**kree**-bah-lo / pore / fah-**boar**

EXPLANATIONS		
This is a *bottle*	Esto es un *bottle*	**ess**-toe / ess / oon / *bottle*
This is called a *bottle*	Esto se llama un *bottle*	**ess**-toe / say / **yah**-mah / oon / *bottle*
It's important that you understand	Es importante qué entienda	ess / eem-pore-**tahn**-tay / kay / en-tee-**en**-dah
Do you have questions?	¿Tiene preguntas?	tee-**en**-ay / pray-**goon**-tahs
Are you certain?	¿Está seguro?	ess-**tah** / say-**goo**-row

ASKING ABOUT FAMILY		
Do you have family?	¿Tiene familia?	tee-**ay**-nay / fah-**mee**-lee-ah
How many children?	¿Cuántos hijos?	**kwahn**-tose / **ee**-hose
How is...	¿Cómo está...	**ko**-mo / ess-**tah**
...your family?	...su familia?	soo / fah-**mee**-lee-ah
...your wife // husband?	...su esposa // su esposo	soo / ess-**po**-sah // soo / ess-**po**-so
...Daughter // Son	Hija // Hijo	**ee**-ha // **ee**-ho
...Mother // Father	Madre // Padre	**mah**-dray // **pah**-dray
...Sister // Brother	Hermana // Hermano	air-**mah**-na // air-**mah**-no
How are your children?	¿Como están sus niños ?	**ko**-mo / ess-**tahn** / soose / **neen**-yos

COMMON TERMS & DIRECTIONS

GOODBYES

Goodbye	Adiós	ah-dee-**ose**
Have a good day	Que le vaya bien	kay / lay / **bah**-yah / bee-**yen**
See you later	Hasta luego	**ah**-stah / loo-**way**-go
See you next week	Hasta la próxima semana	**ah**-stah / lah / **prox**-ee-mah / say-**mah**-nah
See you next time	Hasta la proxima vez	**ah**-stah / lah / **prox**-ee-mah / base
See you tomorrow	Hasta mañana	**ah**-stah / mon-**yah**-nah
Thank you for coming	Gracias por venir	**grah**-see-ahs / pore / beh-**near**

COMMON TERMS

A little // A lot	Un poco // Mucho	oon / **po**-ko // **moo**-cho
Again	Otra vez	**oh**-trah / base
Always // Never	Siempre // Nunca	see-**em**-pray // **noon**-kah
And // Or	Y // O	ee // oh
He // She	Él // Élla	el // **ay**-yah
Here // There	Aquí // Allí	ah-**key** // ah-**yee**
I // You	Yo // Usted	yo // oo-**sted**
More // Less	Más // Menos	mahs // **may**-nose
Welcome	Bienvenidos	bee-en-beh-**nee**-dose

BASIC DIRECTIONS

The rest room is ...	El baño está	el / **bahn**-yo / ess-**tah** ...
- Straight ahead	Derecho	day-**retch**-oh
- in Back // in Front	Atrás // Al frente	ah-**trahs** // ahl / **fren**-tay
Out this door....	Afuera de ésta puerta...	ah-**fwair**-ah / day / **ess**-tah / **p'wear**-tah
- to the Left	- a la izquierda	ah / lah / ease-key-**air**-dah
- to the Right	- a la derecha	ah / lah / day-**retch**-ah
Upstairs // Downstairs	Arriba // Abajo	ahr-**ree**-bah // ah-**bah**-ho
Outside // Inside	Afuera // Adentro	ah-**fway**-rah // ah-**den**-tro
Over there *(point)*	Para allá	**pah**-rah / ah-**yah**
Right here *(point)*	Aquí	ah-**key**

NUMBERS & MEASURES

0	cero	**sair**-oh	19	diecinueve	dee-ess-ee-**nway**-bay
1	uno	**oo**-no	20	veinte	**bane**-tay
2	dos	dose	21	veintiuno	bane-tee-**oo**-no
3	tres	trace	30	treinta	**train**-tah
4	cuatro	**kwah**-tro	32	treinta y dos	**train**-tah / ee / dose
5	cinco	**seen**-ko	40	cuarenta	kwah-**ren**-tah
6	seis	sayce	43	cuarenta y tres	kwah-**ren**-tah / ee / trace
7	siete	see-**et**-tay	50	cincuenta	seen-**kwen**-tah
8	ocho	**oh**-cho	60	sesenta	seh-**sen**-tah
9	nueve	**nway**-bay	65	sesenta y cinco	seh-**sen**-tah / ee / **seen**-ko
10	diez	dee-**ess**	70	setenta	seh-**ten**-tah
11	once	**own**-say	76	setenta y seis	seh-**ten**-tah / ee / sayce
12	doce	**doe**-say	80	ochenta	oh-**chen**-tah
13	trece	**trace**-say	87	ochenta y siete	oh-**chen**-tah / ee / see-**et**-tay
14	catorce	ka-**tore**-say	90	noventa	no-**ben**-tah
15	quince	**keen**-say	98	noventa y ocho	no-**ben**-tah / ee / **oh**-cho
16	dieciseis	dee-ess-ee-**sayce**	100	cien	see-**en**
17	diecisiete	dee-ess-ee-see-**et**-tay	101	ciento uno	see-**en**-toe / **oo**-no
18	dieciocho	dee-ess-ee-**oh**-cho	200	doscientos	dose-see-**en**-tose

ORDINAL NUMBERS

First	Primero	pree-**mare**-oh
Second	Segundo	say-**goon**-doe
Third	Tercero	tair-**sair**-oh

MEASUREMENTS & MEASURES

Inch // inches	Pulgada // Pulgadas	pool-**gah**-dah // pool-**gah**-dahs
Foot // feet	Un pie // Pies	oon / pee-**ay** // pee-**ess**
Gallon	Galón	gah-**loan**
Liter	Litro	**lee**-tro
Pint	Pinta	**peen**-tah
Quart	Cuarto	**kwahr**-toe
Cup	Taza	**tah**-sah
Teaspoon	Cucharadita	koo-chah-rah-**dee**-tah
Tablespoon	Cucharada	koo-chah-**rah**-dah

TIME & TIMING

Yesterday	Ayer	ah-**yair**
Today	Hoy	oy (h is silent)
This morning	Esta mañana	**ess**-tah / mon-**yah**-nah
This afternoon	Esta tarde	**ess**-tah / **tar**-day
Tonight	Esta noche	**ess**-tah / **no**-chay
Tomorrow	Mañana	mahn-**yah**-nah
Tomorrow morning	Mañana por la mañana	mahn-**yah**-nah /pore / lah/ mahn-**yah**-nah
Tomorrow afternoon	Mañana por la tarde	mahn-**yah**-nah / pore / lah / **tar**-day
Tomorrow evening	Mañana por la noche	mahn-**yah**-nah / pore / lah / **no**-chay
This week	Esta semana	**ess**-tah / say-**mah**-nah
Next week	La próxima semana	lah / **prox**-ee-mah / say-**mah**-nah
Next month	El próximo mes	el / **prox**-ee-mo / mace
Right now	Ahora mismo	ah-**oar**-ah / **mees**-mo
Later	Más tarde	mahs // **tar**-day

TELLING TIME

It is…	Son las…	sohn / lahs
At…	A las …	ah / lahs …
Finish it by...	Termínelo a las...	tair-**mee**-nay-lo / ah / lahs
9:00 (AM)	Nueve (por la mañana)	**nway**-bay / pore / lah / mahn-**yah**-nah
9:00 Sharp	Nueve en punto	**nway**-bay / en / **poon**-toe
9:30 (AM)	Nueve y media (...)	**nway**-bay / ee / **may**-dee-ah
Noon	Mediodía	may-dee-oh-**dee**-ah
2:00 (PM)	Dos (por la tarde)	dose (pore / lah / **tar**-day)
2:15 (PM)	Dos y cuarto (...)	dose / ee / **kwahr**-toe (...)
2:45 (PM)	Dos menos cuarto (...)	dose / **may**-nose / **kwahr**-toe (…)
Midnight	Medianoche	may-dee-ah-**no**-chay
Finish it in…	Termínelo en…	tair-**mee**-nay-lo / en
15 minutes	15 minutos	**keen**-say / mee-**noo**-tose
2 hours	2 horas	dose / **oar**-ahs

DAYS – MONTHS – COLORS

DAYS OF THE WEEK		
On…	El…	el
Sunday	domingo	doe-**mean**-go
Monday	lunes	**loo**-ness
Tuesday	martes	**mar**-tess
Wednesday	miércoles	mee-**air**-ko-less
Thursday	jueves	**hway**-bess
Friday	viernes	bee-**air**-ness
Saturday	sábado	**sah**-bah-doe

MONTHS		
In…	En…	en
January	enero	en-**air**-oh
February	febrero	feh-**brair**-oh
March	marzo	**mar**-so
April	abril	ah-**breel**
May	mayo	**my**-oh
June	junio	**hoon**-ee-oh
July	julio	**hool**-ee-oh
August	agosto	ah-**go**-sto
September	septiembre	sep-tee-**em**-bray
October	octubre	oak-**too**-bray
November	noviembre	no-bee-**em**-bray
December	diciembre	dee-see-**em**-bray

COLORS		
Color	Color	ko-**lore**
Black	Negro	**nay**-gro
Blue	Azul	ah-**sool**
Brown	Café	kah-**fay**
Clear	Transparente	trahn-spa-**ren**-tay
Grey	Gris	**grease**
Green	Verde	**bear**-day
Orange	Anaranjado	ah-nah-ron-**ha**-doe
Pink	Rosa OR Rosado/a	**ro**-sah OR ro-**sah**-doe/dah
Purple	Morado	mo-**rah**-doe
Red // Red (wine)	Rojo // Tinto	**ro**-ho / **teen**-toe
Yellow	Amarillo	ah-mah-**ree**-yo
White	Blanco	**blahn**-ko

INTERVIEWING APPLICANTS

INTRODUCTORY QUESTIONS

English	Spanish	Pronunciation
Have you worked in a restaurant before?	¿Ha trabajado en un restaurante antes?	ah / trah-bah-**hah**-doe / en / oon / rest-oh-**ron**-tay / **ahn**-tess
What days can you work?	¿Cuáles días puede trabajar?	**kwahl**-ess / **dee**-ahs / **pway**-day / trah-bah-**har**
What hours can you work?	¿Que horas puede trabajar?	**kay** / **oar**-ahs / **pway**-day / trah-bah-**har**
Can you work...	¿Puede trabajar...	**pway**-day / trah-bah-**har**
...mornings?	...en las mañanas?	en / lahs / mon-**yah**-nahs
...afternoons?	...en las tardes?	en / lahs / **tar**-days
...evenings?	... en las noches?	en / lahs / **no**-chess
...late at night?	...tarde en la noche?	**tar**-day / en / lah / **no**-chay
Do you have transportation?	¿Tiene transporte?	tee-**en**-ay / trans-**pore**-tay

GETTING PERSONAL INFORMATION

English	Spanish	Pronunciation
Fill out our application	Llene usted nuestro aplicación	**yen**-nay / **oo**-sted / **nway**-stro / ah-plee-kah-see-**own**
What is your...	¿Cuál es su...	**kwahl** / ess / soo...
...complete name?	...nombre completo?	**nohm**-bray / comb-**play**-toe
...address?	...dirección?	dee-**reck**-see-own
...city & state?	...ciudad y estado?	see-oo-**dahd** / ee / ess-**tah**-doe
...zip code?	...código postal?	**ko**-dee-go / po-**stahl**
...date of birth?	...fecha de nacimiento?	**fay**-chah / day / nah-see-mee-**en**-toe
...telephone number?	...número de teléfono?	**noo**-may-ro / day / tay-**lay**-fo-no
...social security #?	...número de seguro social	**noo**-may-ro / day / say-**goo**-ro / so-see-**ahl**
...tax ID number?	...número de identidad de impuesto?	**noo**-may-ro / day / ee-den-tee-**dahd** / day eem-**pwess**-toe
You must take ___	Tiene que tomar ___	tee-**en**-ay / kay / toe-**mar** /
- a physical exam	- un examen físico	oon / ex-**ah**-men / **fee**-see-ko
- a drug test	- un examen de drogas	oon / ex-**ah**-men / day / **droh**-gahs
Come back tomorrow	Regrese mañana	ray-**gray**-say / mon-**yah**-nah
...at (time)	...a las (time)	ah / lahs (time)
I will call you ...	Lo voy a llamar...	lo / boy / ah / yah-**mar**
...tomorrow	...mañana	mon-**yah**-nah
...in a few days	...en unos días	en / **oo**-nose / **dee**-ahs

HIRING - PAY - FIRING

VERIFYING INFORMATION

I need to see your...	Necesito ver su...	nay-say-**see**-toe / bear / soo
...social security card	...tarjeta de seguro social	tar-**hay**-tah / day / say-**goo**-ro / so-see-**ahl**
...driver's license	...licencia de manejar	lee-**sen**-see-ah / day / mon-ay-**har**
...resident alien card	...tarjeta verde OR tarjeta de residencia	tar-**hay**-tah / **bear**-day *(green card)* tar-**hay**-tah / day / ray-see-den-**see**-ah
...immigration papers	...documentos de inmigración	doe-koo-**men**-toes / day / een-mee-grah-see-**own**

HIRING - PAY - JOB SCHEDULE

You are hired	Está empleado	ess-**tah** / em-play-**ah**-doe
Start on <u>Friday</u>	Empiece el <u>viernes</u>	em-pee-**ay**-say / el / bee-**air**-ness
Your boss is...	Su jefe es...	soo / **heh**-fay / ess...
You will be paid...	Recibirá su pago...	ray-see-bee-**rah** / soo / **pah**-go
...by check	...por cheque	pore / **check**-ay
...$8 per hour	...$8 dólares por hora	**oh**-cho / **doe**-lah-ress / pore / **oar**-ah
...every Friday	...cada viernes	**kah**-dah / bee-**air**-ness
...every 2 weeks	...cada dos semanas	**kah**-dah / dose / say-**mah**-nahs
...twice a month	...cada quincena	**kah**-dah / keen-**say**-nah
Your schedule will be...	Su horario será...	soo / oar-**ah**-ree-oh / sair-**ah**
Your job will be...	Su trabajo será...	soo / trah-**bah**-ho / sair-**ah**
... dishwasher	... lavaplatos	lah-bah-**plah**-toes
... cook	... cocinero	ko-see-**nair**-oh
... server or waiter	... mesero // mesera	may-**say**-ro // may-**say**-rah
... assistant server	... mesero asistente	may-**say**-ro / ah-cease-**ten**-tay
... cleanup	... limpiar	leem-**pee**-ahr

POOR PERFORMANCE

You are warned	Está sancionado	ess-**tah** / sahn-see-oh-**nah**-doe
You are suspended	Está suspendido	ess-**tah** / soose-pen-**dee**-doe
You are fired	Está despedido	ess-**tah** / dess-pay-**dee**-doe

JOB CONFLICTS & TELEPHONE CALLS

USING THE PHONE

English	Spanish	Pronunciation
Hello, is Maria there?	Bueno, ¿está Maria?	bway-noh / ess-tah / Maria
I'm (your name)	Soy (your name)	soy (your name)
- from (restaurant name)	- de (restaurant name)	day (restaurant name)
He (she) is not here	Él (ella) no está aquí	el (ay-yah) / no / ess-tah / ah-key
Do you want to leave a message?	¿Quiere dejar un recado?	key-air-ay / day-har / oon / ray-kah-doe
No, have her call me	No, que me llame por	no / kay / may / yah-may / pore / fah-boar
I will call back later	Llamo más tarde	yah-mo / mahs / tar-day
My number is . . .	Mi número es . . .	mee / noo-may-ro / ess

COMMON EXCUSES

English	Spanish	Pronunciation
I cannot work today	No puedo trabajar hoy	no / pway-doe / trah-bah-har / oy
I am sick (M/F)	Estoy enfermo (enferma)	ess-toy / en-fair-mo (en-fair-mah)
I am hurt (M/F)	Estoy lesionado (lesionada)	ess-toy / lay-see-oh-nah-do (lay-see-oh-nah-dah)
My child is sick (M/F)	Mi niño (niña) está enfermo (enferma)	mee / neen-yo (neen-yah) / ess-tah / en-fair-mo (en-fair-mah)
My car won't start	Mi carro está dañado	mee / car-rho / ess-tah / dahn-ya-do
There is an emergency	Hay una emergencia	eye / oo-nah / em-air-hen-see-ah
I am going to Mexico	Voy a México	boy / ah / may-hee-ko
I will be back in 5 days	Regreso en 5 días	ray-gray-so / en / seen-ko / dee-ahs

COMMON QUESTIONS & RESPONSES

English	Spanish	Pronunciation
Why aren't you here?	¿Por qué no está aquí?	pore / kay / no / ess-tah / ah-key
Will you be here today?	¿Vendrá hoy?	ben-drah / oy
When will you be back?	¿Cuándo regresará?	kwahn-do / ray-gray-sah-rah
Are you better?	¿Está mejor?	ess-tahs / may-hore
This is not a valid excuse	Esta excusa no es válida	ess-tah / ex-coo-sah / no / ess / bah-lee-dah
You cannot miss work	No puede faltar	no / pway-day / fall-tahr

RULES & EXPECTATIONS

PERSONAL HABITS

YOU MUST...	TIENE QUE...	tee-en-ay / kay
...be on time	...llegar a tiempo	yay-gar / ah / tee-em-po
...be very clean	...estar muy limpio	ess-tar / mwee / leem-pee-oh
...shower before work	...ducharse antes de trabajar	doo-char-say / ahn-tess / day / trah-bah-har
...have clean clothes	...mantener la ropa limpia	mahn-ten-air / lah / ro-pah / leem-pee-ah
...have a clean uniform	...mantener el uniforme limpio	mahn-ten-air / el / oo-nee-for-may / leem-pee-oh
...call if you cannot work	...llamar si no puede venir al trabajo	yah-mar / see / no / pway-day / bay-neer / ahl / trah-bah-hoe
...be courteous to customers	...ser cortes con la clientela	sair / core-tess / cone / lah / klee-en-tay-lah
...be friendly at work	...ser amable en el trabajo	sair / ah-mah-blay / en / el / trah-bah-ho
...do a good job	...hacer un buen trabajo	ah-sair / oon / bwen / trah-bah-ho
...tell me if you have a problem	...avisarme si tiene un problema	ah-bee-sar-may / see / tee-en-ay / oon / pro-blay-mah
...tell me if you don't understand	...avisarme si no entiende	ah-bee-sar-may / see / no / en-tee-en-day

GENERAL & PARKING RULES

No eating	Prohibido comer	pro-ee-bee-doe / koh-mare
No drinking	Prohibido beber	pro-ee-bee-doe / bay-bear
No smoking	Prohibido fumar	pro-ee-bee-doe / foo-mar
No drugs	No tomar drogas	no / toe-mar / droh-gahs
Don't park here	No estacione aquí	no / ess-tah-see-own-ay / ah-key
Don't park there	No estacione allá	no / ess-tah-see-own-ay / ah-yah
Don't park on the left	No estacione a la mano izquierda	no / ess-tah-see-own-ay / ah / lah / mah-no / ease-key-air-dah
Don't park on the right	No estacione a la mano derecha	no / ess-tah-see-own-ay / ah / lah / mah-no / day-ray-chah
Park in the front	Estacione al frente	ess-tah-see-own-ay / ahl / fren-tay
Park in the back	Estacione atrás	ess-tah-see-own-ay / ah-trahs
Park over there (point)	Estacione allá	ess-tah-see-own-ay / ah-yah
Move your car (truck)	Mueva su carro (camión)	mway-bah / soo / car-rho (kah-mee-own)

FOOD & PERSONAL SAFETY

PERSONAL SAFETY		
Be careful!	¡Tenga cuidado!	ten-gah / kwee-**dah**-doe
Call 9-1-1!	¡Llame a nueve uno uno!	**yah**-may / **nway**-bay / **oo**-no / **oo**-no
Call an ambulance	¡Llame a una ambulancia!	**yah**-may / ah / **oo**-nah / ahm-boo-**lahn**-see-ah
Danger!	¡Peligro!	pell-**lee**-gro
Fast! // Hurry!	¡Rápido! // ¡Apúrese!	**rah**-pee-doe // ah-**poo**-ray-say
First Aid Kit	Botiquín de primeros auxilios	bo-tee-**keen** / day / pree-**mare**-ose / ox-**ee**-lee-ose
Get help!	¡Busque ayuda!	**boo**-skay / ah-**you**-dah
Help! // Fire!	¡Socorro! // ¡Fuego!	so-**core**-roh // **fway**-go
Stop now!	¡Pare ahora!	**pah**-ray / ah-**oar**-ah
That's dangerous!	¡Eso es peligroso!	**ess**-so / ess / pell-lee-**grow**-so
That's very sharp	¡Eso es muy agudo!	**ess**-so / ess / mwee / ah-**goo**-doe
That's very sharp	¡Eso es muy filoso!	**ess**-so / ess / mwee / fee-**low**-so
Turn it off!	¡Apáguelo!	ah-**pah**-gay-lo
Turn it on!	¡Enciéndalo!	en-see-**en**-dah-lo
You need a hairnet	Necesita una redicilla para el cabello	nay-say-**see**-tah / **oo**-nah / ray-day-**see**-yah / **pah**-rah / el / kah-**bay**-yo
You need gloves	Necesita guantes	nay-say-**see**-tah / **gwahn**-tess
Wet floor	Piso mojado	**pee**-so / mo-**hah**-doe
FOOD SAFETY		
Always wash your hands…	Siempre debe lavarse las manos...	see-**em**-pray / **day**-bay / lah-**bar**-say / lahs / **mah**-nose…
- after putting out the trash	después de sacar la basura	dess-**pwess** / day / sah-**kar** / lah / bah-**soo**-rah
- after using the bathroom	después de usar el baño	dess-**pwess** / day / oo-**sar** / el / **bahn**-yo
Everything must be clean	Todo debe estar limpio	**toe**-doe / **deh**-bay / ess-**tar** / **leem**-pee-oh
Food must always be clean	La comida debe estar siempre limpia	lah / ko-**mee**-dah / **deh**-bay / ess-**tar** / see-**em**-pray / **leem**-pee-ah
Plates and glasses must always be clean	Los platos y vasos deben estar siempre limpios	lohs / **plah**-tohs / ee / **bah**-sose / **day**-ben / ess-**tar** / see-em-pray / **leem**-pee-ose
Use a band-aid if you cut yourself	Use una curita si se corta	**oo**-say / **oo**-nah / koo-**ree**-tah / see / say / **core**-tah
Utensils must always be clean	Los utensilios deben estar siempre limpios	lohs / oo-ten-**see**-lee-ose / **day**-ben / ess-**tar** / see-em-pray / **leem**-pee-ose
Wash your hands well	Lávese las manos bien	**lah**-bay-say / lahs / **mah**-nose / bee-**en**

DIRECTIONS & ORDERS

WORKING WITH SOMEONE

Bring me the...	Traígame el...	**try**-gah-may / el
Come over here	Venga aquí	**ben**-gah / ah-**key**
Come with me	Venga conmigo	**ben**-gah / cone-**mee**-go
Get me the…	Tráeme el…	**trah**-ay-may / el
Give me a hand	Ayúdeme	ah-**you**-day-may
Go to the store	Váya a la tienda	**bah**-yah / ah / lah / tee-**en**-dah
Hand me the…	Déme el...	**deh**-may / el…
Help him (her)	Ayúdelo (Ayúdela)	ah-**you**-day-lo (ah-**you**-day-lah)
Leave it alone	Déjelo	**deh**-hay-lo
Pick it up	Levántelo	lay-**bahn**-tay-lo
Put it away	Guárdelo	**gwahr**-day-lo
Put it down here	Déjelo aquí	**day**-hay-lo / ah-**kee**
Put it there	Póngalo allí	**pone**-gah-lo / ah-**yee**
Throw it in the trash	Tírelo a la basura	**tee**-ray-lo / ah / lah / bah-**soo**-rah
Use this	Use esto	**oo**-say / **ess**-toe

WORK QUALITY & ENCOURAGEMENT

Do a good job	Haga un buen trabajo	ah-gah / oon / bwen / trah-**bah**-ho
Do it over	Hágalo de nuevo	**ah**-gah-lo / day / **nway**-bo
Good work!	¡Buen trabajo!	bwen / trah-**bah**-ho
Perfect !	¡Perfecto!	pair-**feck**-toe
That's great	Está muy bien.	ess-**tah** / mwee / bee-**en**
That's (not) OK	(No) está bien	(no) ess-**tah** / bee-**en**

TIMING & PRIORITIES

Do it later	Hágalo mas tarde	**ah**-gah-lo / mahs / **tar**-day
Do it now	Hágalo ahora	**ah**-gah-lo / ah-**oar**-ah
Do it quickly	Hágalo rápido	**ah**-gah-lo / **rah**-pee-doe
Finish it today	Termínelo hoy	tair-**mee**-nay-lo / oy
Finish it tomorrow	Termínelo mañana	tair-**mee**-nay-lo / mon-**yah**-nah
Work faster	Trabaje más rápido	trah-**bah**-hay / mahs / **rah**-pee-doe

EVERYDAY QUESTIONS

ONE WORD QUESTIONS

How?	¿Cómo?	ko-mo
How much?	¿Cuánto?	kwahn-toe
How many?	¿Cuántos?	kwahn-tose
Who?	¿Quién?	key-en
What?	¿Qué?	kay
When?	¿Cuándo?	kwahn-doe
Where?	¿Dónde?	doan-day
Why?	¿Por qué?	pore / kay
Whose?	¿De quién?	day / key-en
Which?	¿Cuál?	kwahl

EVERYDAY QUESTIONS

Are you finished?	¿Está terminado?	ess-tah / tair-mee-nah-doe
Can you start today?	¿Puede empezar hoy?	pway-day / em-pay-sahr / oy
Do you understand?	¿Comprende?	comb-pren-day
How long will it take?	¿Cuánto tiempo?	kwahn-toe / tee-em-po
What did you say?	¿Cómo?	ko-mo
What do you need?	¿Qué necesita?	kay / nay-say-see-tah
What happened here?	¿Qué pasó aquí?	kay / pah-so / ah-key
What is this?	¿Qué es esto?	kay / ess / ess-toe
What's the problem?	¿Cuál es el problema?	kwahl / ess / el / pro-blay-mah
When will you finish?	¿Cuándo terminará?	kwahn-doe / tair-mee-nah-rah

WHERE . . .

Where are you going?	¿Adónde va?	ah-doan-day / bah
Where is it?	¿Dónde está?	doan-day / ess-tah
Where is...?	¿Dónde está...?	doan-day / ess-tah
Where are...?	¿Donde están...?	doan-day / ess-tahn

KITCHEN CLEANUP

CLEANING THE EQUIPMENT

Clean the...	Limpie el (la)...	leem-pee-ay / el (lah)
Rinse the...	Enjuague el (la)...	en-**hwah**-gay / el (lah)
Wash the...	Lave el (la)...	**lah**-bay / el (lah)
Blender	Licuadora	lee-kwah-**door**-ah
Cart	Carrito	car-**ree**-toe
Coffeemaker	Cafetera	kah-fay-**tay**-rah
Equipment	Equipo	ay-**kee**-po
Grater	Moledor	mo-lay-**door**
Grill	Parilla	pah-**ree**-yah
Oven // Range	Horno // Estufa	**oar**-no // ess-**too**-fah
Mixer	Mezcladora	mess-klah-**door**-ah
Pots // Pans	Ollas // Sartenes	**oy**-yahs // sar-**ten**-ess
Serving trays	Charolas // bandejas	cha-**role**-ahs // bon-**day**-hahss
Slicer	Rebanador	ray-bahn-ah-**door**
Table(s)	Mesa(s)	**may**-sah(s)
Tools	Herramientas	air-ah-mee-**en**-tahs
Kitchen	Cocina	ko-**see**-nah
Restaurant	Restaurante	rest-ow-**ron**-tay
Clean....	Limpie	**leem**-pee-ay
...up everything	...todo	**toe**-doe
...up outside	...afuera	ah-**fway**-rah
Sweep the floor	Barra el piso	**bahr**-rah / el **pee**-so
Mop the floor	Lave el piso	**lah**-bay / el / **pee**-so
Run the dishwasher	Use el lavaplatos	**oo**-say / el / lah-bah-**plah**-toes

CLEANUP ITEMS

Broom // Mop	Escoba // Trapeador	ess-**ko**-bah // trah-pay-ah-**door**
Bucket	Balde	**ball**-day
Vacuum cleaner	Aspiradora	ah-spee-rah-**door**-ah
Soap // Water	Jabón // Agua	ha-**bone** // **ah**-gwah
Trash	Basura	bah-**soo**-rah
Trash can	Basurero	bah-soo-**rare**-oh
Trash bags	Bolsas para basura	**bowl**-sahs / **pah**-rah / bah-**soo**-rah
Throw it away	Bótelo	**bo**-tay-lo
Take out the trash	Saque la basura	**sah**-kay / lah / bah-**soo**-rah

COOKING COMMANDS

Bake *(the bread)*	Hornee *(el pan)*	oar-**nay**-ay (el / pahn)
Boil *(the water)*	Hierva *(el agua)*	**yair**-bah (el / **ah**-gwah)
Chop *(the vegetables)*	Pique *(las verduras)*	**pee**-kay (lahs / ber-**doo**-rahs)
Clean it in <u>ten</u> minutes	Límpielo en <u>diez</u> minutos	**leem**-pee-ay-lo / en / dee-**ess** / mee-**noo**-tose
Cook it for <u>five</u> minutes per side	Cocínelo por <u>cinco</u> minutos cada lado	ko-see-nay-low / pore / **seen**-ko / mee-**noo**-tose / **kah**-dah / **lah**-doe
Cook it for <u>eight</u> minutes	Cocínelo por <u>ocho</u> minutos	ko-**see**-nay-lo / pore / **oh**-cho / mee-**noo**-tose
Cut *(the meat)*	Corte *(la carne)*	**core**-tay (lah / **car**-nay)
Drain the oil now	Tire el aceite ahora	**tee**-ray / el / ah-**say**-tay / ah-**oar**-ah
Filter the fryers	Filtre las cazuelas	**feel**-tray / lahs / kah-**sway**-lahs
Finish *(the salads)*	Termíne *(las ensaladas)*	tair-**mee**-nay / (lahs / en-sah-**lah**-dahs)
Finish it	Termínelo	tair-**mee**-nay-low

Fry *(the potatoes)*	Fríe *(las papas)*	free-ay (lahs / **pah**-pahs)
Grill *(the meat)*	Ponga la carne en la parrilla	**pone**-gah / lah / **car**-nay / en / lah / pah-**ree**-yah
Microwave (it)	Pongalo en el microondas	**pone**-gah-lo / en / el / mee-**crone**-dahs
Peel *(the potatoes)*	Pele *(las papas)*	**pay**-lay (lahs/ **pah**-pahs)
Put it in the oven	Pongalo en el horno	**pone**-gah-lo / en / el /**oar**-no
Roast *(the chicken)*	Rostise *(el pollo)*	row-**stee**-say (el **poy**-yo)
Sauté *(the onions)*	Saltee *(las cebollas)*	sahl-**tay**-ay / (lahs / say-**boy**-yahs)
Sear *(the steak)*	Abrase *(el bistek)*	ah-**bra**-say (el / bee-**steck**)
Serve *(the meal)*	Sirva *(la comida)*	**seer**-bah (lah / ko-**mee**-dah)
Slice *(the ham)*	Rebane *(el jamón)*	ray-**bah**-nay (el / hah-**moan**)
Steam *(the fish)*	Ponga al vapor *(el pescado)*	**pone**-gah / ahl / bah-**pore** / el / pess-**kah**-doe
Turn it over in 2 hours	Delo vuelta en dos horas	**day**-low / v'**well**-tah / en / dose / **oar**-ahs

RESTAURANT EQUIPMENT

Bottles	Botellas	bo-**tay**-yahs
Bowls	Platos hondos	**plah**-tohs / **oan**-dose
Can opener	Abrelatas	ah-bray-**lah**-tahs
Cups // Glasses	Tazas // Vasos	**tah**-sahs // **bah**-sose
Dish rack	Escurreplatos	ess-koo-ray-**plah**-toes
Fork	Tenedor	tay-nay-**door**
Fork (meat)	Tenedor grande	tay-nay-**door** / **grahn**-day
Knife	Cuchillo	koo-**chee**-yo
Knife (bread)	Cuchillo de pan	koo-**chee**-yo / day / pahn
Knife (kitchen)	Cuchillo de cocina	koo-**chee**-yo / day / ko-**see**-nah
Ladle	Cucharón	koo-chah-**roan**
Napkins	Servilletas	sair-bee-**yay**-tahs
Peeler	Pelador	pay-lah-**door**
Pepper mill	Pimentero	pee-men-**tair**-oh
Salt shaker	Salero	sah-**lair**-oh
Tablecloth	Mantel	mahn-**tell**

Pitcher	Jarra	**hahr**-rah
Plastic bags	Bolsas de plástico	**bowl**-sahs / day / **plah**-stee-ko
Plastic Containers	Guardadores de plástico	gwahr-dah-**door**-ess / day / **plah**-stee-ko
Plastic Lids	Tapas	**tah**-pahs
Plate(s)	Plato(s)	**plah**-tohs
Saucepan	Cacerola	kah-say-**role**-ah
Spatula	Espátula	ess-**pah**-too-lah
Spoon	Cuchara	koo-**chah**-rah
Spoon (soup)	Cuchara de sopa	koo-**chah**-rah / day / **so**-pah
Spoon (table)	Cuchara de mesa	koo-**chah**-rah / day / **may**-sah
Sugar container	Azucarero	ah-soo-kah-**rare**-oh
Tongs // Turners	Pinzas // Volteadoras	**peen**-sahs // bowl-tay-ah-**door**-ahs

MEAL & BEVERAGE TERMS

GENERAL TERMS		
Breakfast	Desayuno	dess-sah-**yoo**-no
Lunch	Almuerzo // Lonche	ahl-**mwair**-so // **loan**-chay
Dinner	Cena	**say**-nah
Appetizer	Entrada	en-**trah**-dah
Entree	Plato principal	**plah**-toe / preen-**see**-pahl
Dessert	Postre	**po**-stray
Food OR Meal	Comida	ko-**mee**-dah
Italian food	Comida italiana	ko-**mee**-dah / ee-tah-lee-**ahn**-ah
Fast food	Comida rápida	ko-**mee**-dah / rah-**pee**-dah
Here or To Go?	Aquí o Para Llevar	ah-**key** / oh / **pah**-rah / yea-**bar**
Meal // Snack	Comida // Merienda	ko-**mee**-dah // may-ree-**en**-dah
Menu	Menú	may-**noo**
Wine List	Lista de vinos	**lease**-tah / day / **bee**-nose

HOW IT'S COOKED		
Rare	Poco cocida	**po**-ko / ko-**see**-dah
Medium	Medio cocida	**may**-dee-oh / ko-**see**-dah
Well-done	Bien cocida	bee-**en** / ko-**see**-dah
(Very) Spicy	(Muy) Picante	(mwee) pee-**kahn**-tay

BEVERAGES		
Beer // Wine	Cerveza // Vino	sair-**bay**-sah // **bee**-no
Red Wine	Vino tinto	**bee**-no / **teen**-toe
Rosé Wine	Vino roso	**bee**-no / roe-**so**
White wine	Vino blanco	**bee**-no / **blahn**-ko
Coffee // Tea	Café // Té	kah-**fay** // tay
Coffee with milk	Café con leche	kah-**fay** / cone / **leh**-chay
Coffee with cream	Café con crema	kah-**fay** / cone / **kray**-mah
Milk // Cream	Leche // Crema	**leh**-chay // **kray**-mah
Soda // Diet soda	Soda // Soda de dieta	**so**-dah // **so**-dah / day / dee-**ay**-tah

FOOD TERMINOLOGY

BASIC FOODS

Beef // Steak	Carne de res // Bistec	car-nay / day / ress // bee-**steck**
Bread // Butter	Pan // Mantequilla	pahn // mon-tay-**key**-ah
Chicken // Turkey	Pollo // Pavo	poy-yo // **pah**-bo
Eggs // Ham	Huevos // Jamón	hway-bose // hah-**moan**
Fish // Seafood	Pescado // Marisco	pay-**ska**-doe // mah-**ree**-sko
Fruit // Cheese	Fruta // Queso	froo-tah // **kay**-so
Potatoes // Rice	Papas // Arroz	**pah**-pahs // ahr-**rose**
Sausage // Bacon	Salchicha // Tocino	sahl-**chee**-cha // toe-**see**-no
Vegetables	Vegetales OR Verduras	bay-hay-**tah**-less OR bear-**doo**-rahs

SANDWICHES & SNACKS

Cheesesteak	Carne con queso	car-nay / cone / **kay**-so
Cheeseburger	Hamburguesa con queso	ahm-boor-**gay**-sah / cone / **kay**-so
Chicken breast	Pechuga de pollo	pay-**choo**-gah / day / **poy**-yo
French fries	Papas fritas	**pah**-pahs / **free**-tahs
Hamburger	Hamburguesa	ahm-boor-**gay**-sah
Hashbrowns	Papas doradas	**pah**-pahs / doe-**rah**-dahs
Onion Rings	Anillos de cebolla	ah-**nee**-yose / day / say-**boy**-ah
Sandwich	Sándwich	**sawn**-weesh
Soup // Salad	Sopa // Ensalada	**so**-pah // en-sah-**lah**-dah

CONDIMENTS

Barbecue sauce	Salsa de barbacoa	**sahl**-sah / day / bar-bah-**ko**-ah
Green pepper	Chile verde	**chee**-lay / **bear**-day
Ketchup	Ketchup	ketchup
Lettuce	Lechuga	lay-**choo**-gah
Mayonnaise	Mayonesa	my-oh-**ness**-ah
Mushrooms	Hongos	**own**-goes
Mustard	Mostaza	mo-**stah**-sah
Oil & Vinegar	Aceite y Vinagre	ah-**say**-tay / ee / bean-**ah**-gray
Onion	Cebolla	say-**boy**-ah
Pickle	Encurtido OR Pickle	en-koor-**tee**-doe OR **peek**-el
Salad dressing	Aliño	ah-**lean**-yo
Salt // Pepper	Sal // Pimienta	sahl // pee-mee-**en**-tah
Tomato	Tomate	toe-**mah**-tay

FRONT OF THE HOUSE

FOR SPANISH SPEAKING CUSTOMERS		
One moment please	Un momento por favor	oon / mo-**men**-toe / pore / fah-**bore**
What would you like?	Qué desea?	kay / day-**say**-ah
What drink?	Qué refresco?	kay / ray-**frays**-ko
For here or to go?	Para aquí o para llevar?	**pah**-rah / ah-**key** / o / **pah**-rah / yay-**bar**
Do you want...	Quiere....	key-**air**-ay
Do you need...	Necesita...	nay-say-**see**-tah
...a combo meal?	...una comida de combo?	oon-ah / ko-**mee**-dah / day / **kohm**-bo
... silverware?	...cubiertos	koo-bee-**air**-toes
...condiments?	...condimentos?	cone-dee-**men**-toes
...a refill?	...más refresco?	mahs / ray-**fray**-sco
We're out of _ketchup_	No tenemos _ketchup_	no / teh-**nay**-mose / ketchup
Wait here // Wait there	Espere aquí // Espere allí	ess-**pair**-ay / ah-**key** // ess-**pair**-ay / ah-yee
Your total is _$5.30_	Son _cinco con treinta_	sohn / **seen**-ko / cone / **train**-tah
Pay here	Pague aquí	**pah**-gay / ah-**key**
Go to the next window	Vaya a la próxima ventana.	**bye**-yah / ah / lah / **prox**-ee-mah / ben-**tah**-nah
Here is your order	Aquí está su orden	ah-**key** / ess-**tah** / soo / **oar**-den

FOR THE WAIT STAFF		
Set up // Clear....	Arregle // Limpie	ahr-**reg**-lay // **leem**-pee-ay
...this table	...esta mesa	ess-tah / **may**-sah
...that table	...esa mesa	ess-ah / **may**-sah
...table number _5_	...la mesa número _5_	lah / **may**-sah / noo-**mair**-oh / **seen**-ko
Get the _plates_	Traiga _los platos_	**try**-gah / lohs / **plah**-tohs
Put out the _plates_	Ponga _los platos_	**pohn**-gah / lohs / **plah**-tohs
Fill the glasses with _water_	Llene los vasos con _agua_	**yay**-nay / lohs / **bahs**-ohs / cone / ah-gwah
Clear the _plates_	Retire _los platos_	ray-**tear**-ay / lohs / **plah**-toes
They need _bread_	Necesitan _pan_	nay-say-**see**-tahn / pahn
Help the waiter	Ayude al mesero	ah-**you**-day / ahl / may-**say**-ro
Do you need help?	¿Necesita ayuda?	nay-say-**see**-tah / ah-**you**-dah
Let me help you	Déjeme ayudarlo	**day**-hay-may / ah-you-**dar**-lo
I will show you	Le mostraré	lay / mo-strah-**ray**

RESTAURANT – PRACTICE CONVERSATIONS

NOTE: The Spanish speaker's part is in the white lines // The English speaker's part is in the shaded lines

1. Looking for work

Buenas tardes señor	Good afternoon Sir
Buenas tardes. ¿Le puedo ayudar?	Good afternoon. May I help you?
Sí señor. Estoy buscando trabajo	Yes Sir. I'm looking for work
¿Qué tipo?	What type?
Mesera	Waitress
¿Ha trabajado en un restaurante antes?	Have you worked in a restaurant before?
Sí señor	Yes Sir
¿Cuánto tiempo?	For how long?
Tres años	Three years
Excelente, llene nuestra aplicación por favor	Excellent, please fill out our application
Gracias, Lo haré ahora mismo	Thank you, I will do it now

2. Checking Identification

Hola Señora, aquí está mi aplicación	Hello Ma'am, here is my application
Gracias Juan. Necesito ver su tarjeta de seguro social	Thanks Juan. I need to see your social security card
Aquí está	Here it is
¿Y su licencia de manejar?	And your drivers license?
No tengo licencia	I don't have a license
¿Tiene transporte?	Do you have transportation?
Sí, mi hermano maneja	Yes, my brother drives
¿Lo traerá todos los días?	Will he bring you every day?
Sí señora	Yes Ma'am
¿Puede empezar mañana?	Can you start tomorrow at 7:00 AM?
Sí, aquí estaré	Yes, I will be here

3. Your schedule is...

Buenas tardes Ramón	Good afternoon Ramon
Buenas tardes	Good afternoon
Su horario es de cuatro de la tarde a la medianoche. Bill es el jefe de turno	Your schedule is 4:00 PM to midnight. Bill is the shift manager
Sí señora, entiendo	Yes Ma'am, I understand
Debe llamar si no puede venir al trabajo	You must call if you cannot come to work
¿Cuál es el número?	What is the number?
456-7890. Escríbalo por favor	456-7890. Write it down please
Un momento. Bueno, ya terminé. ¿Quién habla español?	Just a minute. OK, I'm finished. Who speaks Spanish?
Pregunte por Ernesto. ¿Alguna pregunta más?	Ask for Ernesto. Any more questions?
No señora. Comprendo todo	No Ma'am. I understand everything

4. Job Conflicts

Bueno. ¿Está Rocco?	Hello. Is Rocco there?
Habla Rocco, ¿es usted María?	Rocco speaking. Maria is that you?
Sí jefe	Yes boss
¿Por qué no está aquí? ¿Algo está mal?	Why aren't you here? Is something wrong?
Sí señor, Mi mamá está muy enferma	Oh yes. My mother is very sick
Lo siento. ¿Vendrá hoy?	I'm sorry. Will you be here today?
No, no puedo trabajar hoy	No, I cannot work today
Está bien. ¿cuándo regresa?	That's fine. When will you be back?
Me voy a México. Regreso en cinco días	I am going to México. I will be back in 5 days
¿Cinco días? Es mucho tiempo	Five days? That's a long time
Sí, lo sé	Yes, I know
Está bien, pero no puede faltar más	It's okay, but you cannot miss more work
Bueno, gracias jefe	OK, thanks boss

5. Food Safety

Tomás, necesito ayuda en la cocina	Tomás, I need some help in the kitchen
Sí señora	Yes Ma'am
Pique las cebollas por favor	Chop the onions please
¡Ah!!! Me corté el dedo; está sangrando	Ahh!!! I cut my finger; it's bleeding
No toque nada Venga conmigo al botiquín	Don't touch anything Come with me to the first aid kit
Sí señora. Necesito una curita	Yes ma'am. I need a band-aid
Debe lavarse las manos y use guantes para protección	You must wash your hands and use gloves for protection
Bueno – ¿Es muy importante?	OK – is this very important?
Sí. Nunca Nunca deje caer sangre cerca de la comida. Es importante que entienda	Yes. Never Never get blood near the food. It is important that you understand
Entiendo y me siento mucho mejor. Gracias	I understand, and I feel much better. Thanks

6. Fast Food Order

Buenas noches. ¿Qué desea?	Good evening. What would you like?
Necesito dos comidas combo, el número tres	I need two combo meals, number three
¿Qué refresco?	What drink?
De dieta Coca-Cola	Diet Coke
¿Algo más?	Anything else?
No, es todo. ¿Cuánto cuesta?	No, that's it. How much is it?
Son diez con treinta - vaya a la próxima ventana	It's $10.30 – go to the next window
Necesito ketchup, por favor.	I need ketchup please.
Si, aquí está su orden, y el ketchup Que tenga un buen día	Ok, here is your order, and the ketchup Have a nice day
Gracias. Lo mismo	Thanks. Same to you

RESTAURANT - PRACTICE CONVERSATIONS

7. Cleaning the Equipment

Hola Jorge. ¿Qué pasa?	Hello Jorge. What's up?
Hola jefa, estoy limpiando la freidora	Hey boss, I'm cleaning the fryer
Perfecto. ¿Puede limpiar la parilla también?	Perfect. Can you clean the grill too?
¿La freidora y la parrilla? Es mucho trabajo	The fryer and the grill? That's a lot of work.
Sara lo ayudará	Sara will help you
OK, ¿algo más?	OK, anything else?
Lave la estufa y saque la basura antes de salir.	Wash the stove and take out the trash before you leave
Bueno - trabajaremos juntos	OK - We'll work together
¿Han terminado?	Have you finished?
Sí jefa – finalmente	Yes ma'am – finally
¡Caramba, qué buen trabajo! Que tenga una buena noche	Wow, great work! Have a good night

8. Prep Cook

Marco, estamos muy ocupados ahora ¿Está listo?	Marco, we're really busy now Are you ready?
Seguro, ¿que sigue?	Sure, what's next?
Primero, ponga la carne en el horno Después rostise los pollos	First, put the meat in the oven Then, roast the chickens
Bueno, Lo haré enseguida	OK, I'll get that done right away
Ponga los vegetales al vapor Y termine las ensaladas	Steam the vegetables And finish the salads
¡Caramba! este es un lugar muy ocupado	Man, this is a busy place
Sí, frite las papas también	Yes, fry the potatoes too

9. Multiple Tasks

Buenas noches Juanita, venga conmigo	Good evening Juanita, come with me
Sí señor. ¿Qué necesita?	Yes Sir. What do you need?
Necesitamos hacer muchas cosas hoy	We need to do many things today
Sí señor, dígame	Yes, sir, tell me
Primero, barra el piso	First, sweep the floor
Bueno, algo más?	OK, anything else?
Después aspire al frente	Then vacuum out front
¿La alfombra?	The carpet?
Sí, haga un buen trabajo y limpie las mesas también	Yes, do a good job and clean the tables too
Está bien señor Martín	All right Mr. Martin
Muchas gracias Juanita	Thank you very much Juanita

Workplace SPANISH®

Directions: Use the information provided in the word bank to complete the Spanish to English translations below.

Importante	Muchas gracias
Español	Inglés
Buenos días	Siempre
Jefe	Preguntas
Buen día	De nada
Trabajo	Jefe de turno
Comprendo	¿Le puedo ayudar?

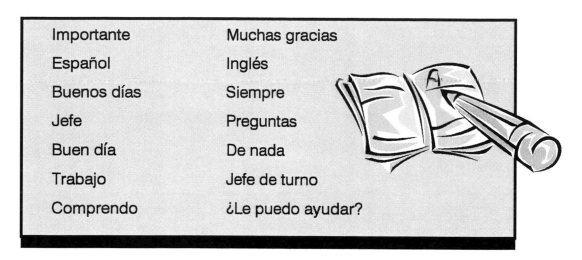

1. Hola, soy el _____. *(Boss)*

2. ¿ _____ _____ _____? *(Can I help you?)*

3. _____ _____, señorita. *(Thank you very much)*

4. Buenas tardes, soy el _____ ____ _____. *(Shift Manager)*

5. Otra vez, por favor. No _____ . *(Understand)*

6. ¿Tiene _____? *(Questions)*

7. Es _____ que entienda. *(Important)*

8. Dígame en _____. *(English)*

9. ¿Está buscando _____? *(Work)*

10. Hablo un poco de _____. *(Spanish)*

DRILLS FOR SKILLS

What would you say...

1. ... to say to an employee who frequently arrives late to work?

_____

2. ... to tell an employee he is doing a good job?

_____

3. ... to remind an employee to shower before work?

_____

4. ... to an employee who wears a dirty uniform?

_____

5. ... to tell employees that they must call if they can't come to work?

_____

<u>6.</u> ... to communicate the importance of reporting a problem ?

_____

7. ... to clarify a location for employee parking?

_____

8. ... to communicate that employees may not eat while working?

_____

9. ... to tell employees that drugs are prohibited?

_____

10. ... to instruct employees that they must be courteous to customers?

_____

D
R
I
L
L
S

F
O
R

S
K
I
L
L
S

Directions: Using the word bank, fill in the spaces provided with the correct Spanish word.

La comida	Caliente	Redecilla
Ropa	Curita	Sangrando
Muy filoso	Mojado	Manos
Zapatos anti-deslizantes	Lávese	Limpio

1. No toque nada si está _____.
   (Bleeding)

2. Siempre _____ las _____.
   (Wash) // *(Hands)*

3. El cuchillo está _____ _____.
   (Very sharp)

4. Use una _____ si se corta.
   (Band-aid)

5. Eso está muy _____.
   (Hot)

6. Tiene que usar una _____.
   (Hairnet)

7. _____ debe estar siempre limpia.
   (Food)

8. Tiene que llevar _____ _____-_____.
   (Slip-resistant shoes)

9. Tenga cuidado. Piso _____.
   (Wet)

10. Todo debe estar siempre _____.
    (Clean)

D R I L L S F O R S K I L L S

Directions: Choose the correct answer.

1. That's great!
    a. ¡Buen Trabajo!
    b. ¡Perfecto!
    c. Está muy bien

2. Slice
    a. Abrase
    b. Pele
    c. Rebane

3. Cook for 8 minutes
    a. Cocínelo por cinco minutos
    b. Cocínelo por ocho minutos
    c. Rostise el pollo

4. Clean the Kitchen
    a. Limpie la cocina
    b. Limpie el carrito
    c. Lave las charolas

5. Do it quickly
    a. Hágalo rápido
    b. Hágalo ahora
    c. Hágalo mas tarde

6. Put it there
    a. Levántelo
    b. Póngalo allí
    c. Guárdelo

7. Bake
    a. Hornee
    b. Rostise
    c. Saltee

8. Throw it away
    a. Levántelo
    b. Guárdelo
    c. Bótelo

9. Sweep the floor
    a. Lave el piso
    b. Barra el piso
    c. Limpie la parrilla

10. Leave it alone
    a. Déjelo
    b. Use esto
    c. Guárdelo

D R I L L S F O R S K I L L S

EQUIPMENT

Directions: Match the English and Spanish statements

1. Spoon	a. Horno	
2. Bolsas de plástico	b. Napkins	
3. Oven	c. Cuchara	
4. Mesa	d. Licuadora	
5. Tenedor	e. Utensilios	
6. Glasses	f. Fork	
7. Utensils	g. Lavaplatos	
8. Servilletas	h. Broom	
9. Charolas	i. Vasos	
10. Escoba	j. Table	
11. Dishwasher	k. Plastic bags	
12. Blender	l. Serving trays	

Answers

1. _____
2. _____
3. _____
4. _____
5. _____
6. _____
7. _____
8. _____
9. _____
10. _____
11. _____
12. _____

DRILLS FOR SKILLS

MEAL AND BEVERAGE TERMS

Directions: Choose the correct answer.

1. Meal
    a. Vino
    b. Comida
    c. Menú

2. Diet soda
    a. Soda
    b. Leche
    c. Soda de dieta

3. Lettuce
    a. Lechuga
    b. Cebolla
    c. Sopa

4. Salad dressing
    a. Aliño
    b. Chile
    c. Ensalada

5. Rare
    a. Picante
    b. Medio cocida
    c. Poco cocida

6. Coffee
    a. Café
    b. Comida
    c. Cena

7. Lunch
    a. Cena
    b. Almuerzo
    c. Postre

8. Spicy
    a. Arroz
    b. Picante
    c. Mostaza

9. Chicken breast
    a. Pechuga de pollo
    b. Tocino
    c. Pescado

10. Mustard
    a. Tomate
    b. Mostaza
    c. Vinagre

DRILLS FOR SKILLS

Directions: Use the captions provided in the picture below to translate the following Spanish phrases.

1. _____ now. *(Do it)*

2. Mañana _____ _____ _____. *(Evening)*

3. En dos _____. *(Hours)*

4. Termínelo a las _____ _____ _____. *(3:30)*

5. Nueve _____ _____. *(Sharp)*

6. La próxima _____. *(Week)*

ANSWERS

Page 32

1. Jefe	2. Le puedo ayudar	3. Muchas gracias	4. Jefe de turno	5. Comprendo
6. Preguntas	7. Importante	8. Inglés	9. Trabajo	10. Español

Page 33

1. Tiene que llegar a tiempo.
2. Hace un buen trabajo.
3. Tiene que ducharse antes de trabajar.
4. Tiene que mantener el uniforme limpio.
5. Tiene que llamar si no puede venir al trabajo.
6. Tiene que avisarnos si tiene un problema.
7. Estacione allá.
8. Prohibido comer.
9. No tomar drogas.
10. Tiene que ser cortés con la clientela.

Page 34

1. Sangrando	2. Lávese // Manos	3. Muy filoso	4. Curita	5. Caliente
6. Redecilla	7. La comida	8. Zapatos anti-deslizantes	9. Mojado	10. Limpio

Page 35

1. C	2. C	3. B	4. A	5. A
6. B	7. A	8. C	9. B	10. A

Page 36

1. C	2. K	3. A	4. J	5. F	6. I
7. E	8. B	9. L	10. H	11. G	12. D

Page 37

1. B	2. C	3. A	4. A	5. C
6. A	7. B	8. B	9. A	10. B

Page 38

1. Hágalo	2. En la noche	3. Horas
4. Tres y media	5. En punto	6. Semana

D
R
I
L
L
S

F
O
R

S
K
I
L
L
S

RESTAURANT - KEYWORD LIST

A little	Un poco	oon / **po**-ko
A lot	Mucho	**moo**-cho
Again	Otra vez	**oh**-trah / base
Always	Siempre	see-**em**-pray
Appetizer	Entrada	en-**trah**-dah
Ask for....	Pregunte por ...	pray-**goon**-tay / pore...
August	Agosto	ah-**go**-sto
Back	Atrás	ah-**trahs**
Bacon	Tocino	toe-**see**-no
Bake	Hornee	oar-**nay**-ay
Barbecue sauce	Salsa de barbacoa	**sahl**-sah / day / bar-bah-**ko**-ah
Beef	Carne de res	**car**-nay / day / ress
Beer	Cerveza	sair-**bay**-sah
Bleeding	Sangrado	sahn-**grah**-doe
Blender	Licuadora	lee-kwah-**door**-ah
Boil (verb)	Hierva	**yair**-bah
Boss	Jefe // Jefa	**heh**-fay // **heh**-fah
Bottles	Botellas	bo-**tay**-yahs
Bowls	Platos hondos	**plah**-toes/ **oan**-does
Bread	Pan	pahn
Breakfast	Desayuno	dess-sah-**yoo**-no
Bring me the...	Traígame el...	**try**-gah-may / el ...
Broom	Escoba	ess-**ko**-bah
Brother	Hermano	air-**mah**-no
Bucket	Balde	**ball**-day
Butter	Mantequilla	mon-tay-**key**-ah
Call (command)	Llame	**yah**-may
Call (noun)	Llamada	yah-**mah**-dah
Call 911!	¡Llame nueve uno uno!	**yah**-may / **nway**-bay / **oo**-no / **oo**-no
Call an ambulance!	¡Llame a una ambulancia!	**yah**-may / ah / **oo**-nah / ahm-boo-**lahn**-see-ah
Can opener	Abrelatas	ah-bray-**lah**-tahs
Careful	Cuidado	kwee-**dah**-doe
Cart	Carrito	car-**ree**-toe
Check (noun)	Cheque	**check**-ay
Cheese	Queso	**kay**-so
Cheeseburger	Hamburguesa con queso	ahm-boor-**gay**-sah / cone / **kay**-so
Cheesesteak	Carne con queso	**car**-nay / cone / **kay**-so
Chicken	Pollo	**poy**-yo
Chicken breast	Pechuga de pollo	pay-**choo**-gah / day / **poy**-yo

Children	Niños/as // Niño/a	**neen**-yos/yahs // **neen**-yo/ya
Chop (verb)	Pique	**pee**-kay
Clean (adjective)	Limpio	**leem**-pee-oh
Clean // Clean it	Límpie // Límpielo	**leem**-pee-ay // **leem**-pee-ay-lo
Clear the dishes	Retire los platos	ray-**tear**-ay / lohs / **plah**-toes
Clothes	Ropa	**ro**-pah
Coffee	Café	kah-**fay**
Coffeemaker	Cafetera	cah-fay-**tay**-rah
Come (command)	Venga	**ben**-gah
Come back (verb)	Regrese	ray-**gray**-say
Condiments	Condimentos	cone-dee-**men**-toes
Cook (noun)	Cocinero	ko-see-**nair**-oh
Cook (verb)	Concíne	ko-**see**-nay
Cream	Crema	**kray**-mah
Cups	Tazas	**tah**-sahs
Cut (verb)	Corte	**core**-tay
Danger!	¡ Peligro!	pell-**lee**-gro
Dangerous	Peligroso	pell-lee-**grow**-so
Daughter	Hija	**ee**-ha
December	Diciembre	dee-see-**em**-bray
Dessert	Postre	**po**-stray
Diet soda	Soda de dieta	**so**-dah / day / dee-**ay**-tah
Dinner	Cena	**say**-nah
Dish rack	Escurreplatos	ess-koo-ray-**plah**-toes
Dishwasher	Lavaplatos	lah-bah-**plah**-toes
Do a good job	Haga un buen trabajo	**ah**-gah / oon / bwen / trah-**bah**-ho
Do it (command)	Hágalo	**ah**-gah-lo
Do it over	Hágalo de nuevo	**ah**-gah-lo / day / **nway**-bo
Do not touch	No toque	no / **toe**-kay
Do you need help?	Necesita ayuda?	nay-say-**see**-tah / ah-**you**-dah
Downstairs	Abajo	ah-**bah**-ho
Driver's license	Licencia de manejar	lee-**sen**-see-ah / day / mon-ay-**har**
Drug test	Examen de drogas	ex-**ah**-men / day / **droh**-gahs
Eggs	Huevos	**hway**-bose
Entree	Plato principal	**plah**-toe / preen-**see**-pahl
Equipment	Equipo	ay-**kee**-po
Everything	Todo	**toe**-doe
Excuse	Excusa	ex-**coo**-sah
Excuse me	Disculpe // Perdone	dee-**school**-pay // pair-**doan**-ay

Fast	Rápido	**rah**-pee-doe
Fast Food	Comida rápida	ko-**mee**-dah / **rah**-pee-dah
Faster	Más rápido	mahs / **rah**-pee-doe
Father	Padre	**pah**-dray
Fill out (command)	Llene	**yay**-nay
Filter (verb)	Filtre	**feel**-tray
Finish it (command)	Termínelo	tair-**mee**-nay-lo
Finished	Terminado	tair-mee-**nah**-doe
Fire!	¡Fuego!	**fway**-go
First Aid Kit	Botiquín de primeros auxilios	bo-tee-**keen** / day / pree-**mare**-ose / ox-**ee**-lee-ose
Fish	Pescado	peh-**ska**-doe
Food	Comida	ko-**mee**-dah
Fork	Tenedor	tay-nay-**door**
Fork (meat)	Tenedor grande	tay-nay-**door** / **grahn**-day
French fries	Papas fritas	**pah**-pahs / **free**-tahs
Friday	Viernes	bee-**air**-ness
Front	Al frente	ahl / **fren**-tay
Fruit	Fruta	**froo**-tah
Fry (verb)	Fríe	**free**-ay
Get help!	¡Busque ayuda!	**boo**-skay / ah-**you**-dah
Get me the…	Tráeme el…	**trah**-ay-may / el …
Give me a hand	Ayúdeme	ah-**you**-day-may
Glasses	Vasos	**bah**-sose
Gloves	Guantes	**gwahn**-tess
Go to the store	Váya a la tienda	**bah**-yah / ah / lah / tee-**en**-dah
Good afternoon	Buenas tardes	**bway**-nahs / **tar**-days
Good evening	Buenas noches	**bway**-nahs / **no**-chess
Good morning	Buenos días	**bway**-nose / **dee**-ahs
Good work!	¡Buen trabajo!	bwen / trah-**bah**-ho
Goodbye	Adiós	ah-dee-**ose**
Grater	Moledor	mo-lay-**door**
Green pepper	Chile verde	**chee**-lay / **bear**-day
Grill (noun)	Parilla	pah-**ree**-yah
Grill (verb)	Ponga a la parilla	**pone**-gah / ah / lah / pah-**ree**-yah
Hairnet	Redecilla	ray-day-**see**-yah
Ham	Jamón	hah-**moan**
Hamburger	Hamburguesa	ahm-boor-**gay**-sah
Hand me the…	Déme el…	**deh**-may / el…
Hashbrowns	Papas doradas	**pah**-pahs / doe-**rah**-dahs
Hello	Hola	**oh**-lah
Help (noun)	Ayuda	ah-**you**-dah

Help him // Help her	Ayúdelo // Ayúdela	ah-**you**-day-lo // ah-**you**-day-lah
Help the waiter.	Ayude al mesero.	ah-**you**-day / ahl / may-**say**-ro
Help! (urgent)	¡Socorro!	so-**core**-oh
Here	Aquí	ah-**key**
How are you?	¿Como está?	**ko**-mo / ess-**tah**
Hurry (command)	Apúrese	ah-**poo**-ray-say
Hurt	Lesionado/a	lay-see-oh-**nah**-doe
Husband	Esposo	ess-**po**-so
I (me)	Yo	yo
I'm the manager (M // F)	Soy el jefe // Soy la jefa	soy / el / **heh**-fay // soy / lah / **heh**-fah
Immigration papers	Documentos de inmigración	doe-koo-**men**-tose / day / een-mee-grah-see-**own**
Inside	Dentro	**den**-tro
Italian food	Comida italiana	ko-**mee**-dah / ee-tah-lee-**ahn**-ah
January	Enero	en-**air**-oh
Job	Trabajo	trah-**bah**-ho
July	Julio	**hool**-ee-oh
June	Junio	**hoon**-ee-oh
Just a minute	Un momento	oon / mo-**men**-toe
Ketchup	Ketchup	ketchup
Kitchen	Cocina	ko-**see**-nah
Knife	Cuchillo	koo-**chee**-yo
Knife (bread)	Cuchillo de pan	koo-**chee**-yo / day / pahn
Knife (kitchen)	Cuchillo de cocina	koo-**chee**-yo / day / ko-**see**-nah
Ladle	Cucharón	koo-chah-**roan**
Later	Luego	loo-**way**-go
Leave it alone	Déjelo	**deh**-hay-lo
Left	Izquierda	ease-key-**air**-dah
Less	Menos	**may**-nose
Let me help you.	Déjeme ayudarlo.	**day**-hay-may / ah-you-**dar**-lo
Lettuce	Lechuga	lay-**choo**-gah
Lunch	Almuerzo // Lonche	ahl-**mwair**-so // **loan**-chay
Manager	Gerente	heh-**ren**-tay
Mayonnaise	Mayonesa	my-oh-**ness**-ah
Meal	Comida	ko-**mee**-dah
Medium	Medio cocida	**may**-dee-oh / ko-**see**-dah
Menu	Menú	may-**noo**
Mexican food	Comida mexicana	ko-**mee**-dah / meck-see-**kah**-nah
Microwave (noun)	Microondas	mee-**crone**-dahs
Microwave (verb)	Ponga al microondas	**pone**-gah / ahl / mee-**crone**-dahs
Milk	Leche	**leh**-chay
Minute	Momento	mo-**men**-toe

Miss // Mrs.	Señorita // Señora	sen-yore-**ree**-tah // sen-**yore**-ah
Mister // Sir	Señor	sen-**yore**
Mixer	Mezcladora	mess-klah-**door**-ah
Mop (command)	Lave	**lah**-bay
Mop (noun)	Trapeador	trah-pay-ah-**door**
More	Más	mahs
Mother	Madre	**mah**-dray
Move (command)	Mueva	**mway**-bah
Mushrooms	Hongos	**own**-goes
Mustard	Mostaza	mo-**stah**-sah
Napkins	Servilletas	sair-bee-**yay**-tahs
Never	Nunca	**noon**-kah
Next month	El próximo mes	el / **prox**-ee-mo / mace
Next week	La próxima semana	lah / **prox**-ee-mah / say-**mah**-nah
Now	Ahora	ah-**oar**-ah
October	Octubre	oak-**too**-bray
Oil *(salad or cooking)*	Aceite	ah-**say**-tay
Onion	Cebolla	say-**boy**-ah
Onion Rings	Anillos de cebolla	ah-**nee**-yose / day / say-**boy**-ah
Outside	Afuera	ah-**fway**-rah
Oven	Horno	**oar**-no
Over there	Para allá	**pah**-rah / ah-**yah**
Pan (s)	Sartén (es)	sar-**ten**-(ess)
Park (command)	Estacione	ess-tah-see-**own**-ay
Peel (verb)	Pele	**pay**-lay
Peeler	Pelador	pay-lah-**door**
Pepper	Pimienta	pee-mee-**en**-tah
Pepper mill	Pimentero	pee-men-**tair**-oh
Perfect!	¡Perfecto!	pair-**feck**-toe
Physical exam	Examen físico	ex-**ah**-men / **fee**-see-ko
Pick it up	Levántelo	lay-**bahn**-tay-lo
Pickle	Encurtido OR Pickle	en-koor-**tee**-doe
Pitcher	Jarra	**hahr**-rah
Plastic bags	Bolsas de plástico	**bowl**-sahs / day / **plah**-stee-ko
Plastic Containers	Guardadores de plástico	gwahr-dah-**door**-ess / day / **plah**-stee-ko
Plastic Lids	Tapas	**tah**-pahs
Plate(s)	Plato(s)	**plah**-toh(s)
Please	Por favor	pore / fah-**boar**
Potatoes	Papas	**pah**-pahs
Pots	Ollas	**oy**-yahs
Put (command)	Póngalo	**pone**-gah-lo
Put it away	Guárdelo	**gwahr**-day-lo

Put it down	Déjelo	**day**-hay-lo
Quickly	Rápido	**rah**-pee-doe
Range	Estufa	ess-**too**-fah
Rare	Poco cocida	**po**-ko / ko-**see**-dah
Refill	Más refresco	mahs / ray-**frays**-ko
Repeat that	Repita eso	ray-**pee**-tah / **ess**-oh
Resident alien card (green card)	Tarjeta de residencia	tar-**hay**-tah / day / ray-see-dense-**ee**-ah
Restaurant	Restaurante	rest-oh-**ron**-tay
Rice	Arroz	ahr-**rose**
Right	Derecha	day-**retch**-ah
Right here	Aquí	ah-**key**
Right now	Ahora mismo	ah-**oar**-ah / **mees**-mo
Rinse (command)	Enjuague	en-**hwah**-gay
Roast	Rostise	row-**stee**-say
Run the dishwasher	Use el lavaplatos	**oo**-say / el / lah-bah-**plah**-tose
Salad	Ensalada	en-**sah**-lah-dah
Salad Dressing	Aliño	ah-**lean**-yo
Salt	Sal	sahl
Salt shaker	Salero	sah-**lair**-oh
Salty	Salado	sah-**lah**-doe
Sandwich	Sándwich	**sahn**-weesh
Saturday	Sábado	**sah**-bah-doe
Saucepan	Cacerola	kah-say-**role**-ah
Sausage	Salchicha	sahl-**chee**-cha
Sauté (verb)	Saltee	sahl-**tay**-ay
Schedule	Horario	oar-**ah**-ree-oh
Seafood	Marisco	mah-**ree**-sko
Sear (verb)	Abrase	ah-**brah**-say
Serve	Sirva	**seer**-bah
Server	Mesero // Mesera	meh-**say**-ro // meh-**say**-rah
Server's assistant	Mesero Asistente	may-**say**-ro / ah-cease-**ten**-tay
Serving trays	Charolas OR bandejas	cha-**role**-ahs, bon-**day**-hahss
Set up	Arregle	ahr-**reg**-lay
Sharp	Agudo OR Filoso	ah-**goo**-doe OR fee-**low**-so
Shift	Turno	**tour**-no
Shift manager	Jefe de turno	**heh**-fay / day / **tour**-no
Shower (verb)	Ducharse	doo-**char**-say
Sick	Enfermo/a	en-**fair**-mo
Sit down (command)	Siéntese	see-**en**-tay-say
Sister	Hermana	air-**mah**-na
Slice (verb)	Rebane	ray-**bah**-nay
Slicer	Rebanador	ray-bahn-ah-**door**

Snack	Merienda	may-ree-**en**-dah
Soap	Jabón	ha-**bone**
Social security card	Tarjeta de seguro social	tar-**hay**-tah / day / say-**goo**-ro / so-see-**ahl**
Social Security Number	Número de seguro social	**noo**-may-row / day / say-**goo**-ro / so-see-**ahl**
Soda	Soda	**so**-dah
Son	Hijo	**ee**-ho
Soup	Sopa	**so**-pah
Spatula	Espátula	ess-**pah**-too-lah
Spicy	Picante	pee-**cahn**-tay
Spoon	Cuchara	koo-**chah**-rah
Spoon (soup)	Cuchara de sopa	koo-**chah**-rah / day / **so**-pah
Spoon (table)	Cuchara de mesa	koo-**chah**-rah / day / **may**-sah
Spring	Primavera	pree-mah-**bear**-ah
Steak	Bistec	bee-**steck**
Steam (verb)	Ponga al vapor	**pone**-gah / ahl / bah-**pore**
Stop (command)	Pare	**pah**-ray
Straight ahead	Directo	dee-**reck**-toe
Sugar container	Azucarero	ah-soo-kah-**rare**-oh
Summer	Verano	bear-**ah**-no
Sunday	Domingo	doe-**mean**-go
Sweep (command)	Barra	**bahr**-rah
Table(s)	Mesa(s)	**may**-sah(s)
Tablecloth	Mantel	mahn-**tell**
Take out the trash	Saque la basura	**sah**-kay / lah / bah-**soo**-rah
Tea	Té	tay
Telephone number	Número de teléfono	**noo**-may-ro / day / tay-**lay**-fo-no
Tell me	Dígame	**dee**-gah-may
Thank you (very much)	(Muchas) gracias	(**moo**-chahs) **grah**-see-ahs
That's great	Está muy bien	ess-**tah** / mwee / bee-**en**
That's not OK	No está bien	no / ess-**tah** / bee-en
That's OK	Está bien	ess-**tah** / bee-en
There	Allí	ah-**yee**
They need ...	Necesitan...	nay-say-**see**-tahn
This afternoon	Esta tarde	**ess**-tah / **tar**-day
This morning	Esta mañana	**ess**-tah / mon-**yah**-nah
This week	Esta semana	**ess**-tah / say-**mah**-nah
Throw it away	Tírelo a la basura	**tee**-ray-lo / ah / lah / bah-**soo**-rah
Today	Hoy	oy
To Go (take food out)	Para Llevar	**pah**-rah / yea-**bar**
Tomato	Tomate	toe-**mah**-tay
Tomorrow	Mañana	mahn-**yah**-nah

Tomorrow afternoon	Mañana en la tarde	mahn-**yah**-nah / en / lah / **tar**-day
Tomorrow evening	Mañana en la noche	mahn-**yah**-nah / en / lah / **no**-chay
Tomorrow morning	Mañana en la mañana	mahn-**yah**-nah / en / lah / mon-**yah**-nah
Tongs	Pinzas	**peen**-sahs
Tonight	Esta noche	**ess**-tah / **no**-chay
Tools	Herramientas	air-ah-mee-**en**-tahs
Trash	Basura	bah-**soo**-rah
Trash bags	Bolsas para basura	**bowl**-sahs / **pah**-rah / bah-**soo**-rah
Trash can	Basurero	bah-soo-**rare**-oh
Turkey	Pavo	**pah**-bo
Turn it off	Apáguelo	ah-**pah**-gay-lo
Turn it on	Enciéndalo	en-see-**en**-dah-lo
Turn it over	Delo vuelta	day-low / v'well-tah
Turners	Volteadoras	bowl-tay-ah-door-ahs
Uniform	Uniforme	oo-nee-for-may
Upstairs	Arriba	ahr-ree-bah
Use this	Use esto	oo-say/ ess-toe
Utensils	Utensilios	oo-ten-**see**-lee-ose
Vacuum cleaner	Aspiradora	ah-spee-rah-**door**-ah
Vegetables	Vegetales OR Verduras	bay-hay-**tah**-less OR bear-**door**-ahs
Very well	Muy bien	mwee / bee-**en**
Vinegar	Vinagre	bean-**ah**-gray
Wash (command)	Lave	**lah**-bay
Wash your hands	Lávese las manos	**lah**-bay-say / lahs / **mah**-nose
Water	Agua	**ah**-gwah
Week	Semana	say-**mah**-nah
Well-done	Bien cocida	bee-**en** / ko-**see**-dah
Wet floor	Piso mojado	**pee**-so / mo-**hah**-doe
Wife	Esposa	ess-**po**-sah
Wine	Vino	**bee**-no
Wine List	Lista de vinos	**lease**-tah / day / **bee**-nose
Winter	Invierno	een-bee-**air**-no
Work (noun)	Trabajo	trah-**bah**-ho
Work (verb)	Trabajar	trah-bah-**har**
Write it	Escríbalo	ess-**kree**-bah-lo
Yesterday	Ayer	ah-**yair**
You're fired	Está despedido	ess-**tah** / dess-pay-**dee**-doe
You're suspended	Está suspendido	ess-**tah** / soose-pen-**dee**-doe
You're warned	Está sancionado	ess-**tah** / sahn-see-oh-**nah**-doe
You're welcome	De nada	day / **nah**-dah

FOR NEW EXPRESSIONS

YOUR SUGGESTIONS & FEEDBACK

We appreciate your purchase of this manual and CD, and hope it will help you to improve communication with Spanish speakers at your workplace. Your suggestions and comments are very important to us. Please take a minute to answer the questions and fax this form back to us. Gracias.

1. Did you find our materials easy to use?   _____ yes   ___ no
Comments:

2. Are there additional expressions we should add to the manual?
Please list them:

3. Will our materials help you communicate with Spanish speakers on the job?   _____ yes   ___ no

4. Any suggestions:

5. Would you like us to contact you regarding customized Workplace Spanish® training materials?
   ____ yes   (please give us your phone number:)

Please tell us:

Name of Program Used:

Your Name:

Your e-mail address:

If you had Spanish training classes, who taught the classes?

a) Organization that did the teaching:

b) Instructor's Name:

PLEASE FAX TO: (866) 772-0228 (NO COVER SHEET NECESSARY)

THANK YOU FOR YOUR FEEDBACK!